The
Growing
Discontent
of the
Masses

Three Essays on the Social Condition

Emma Goldman

*'On Patriotism' published 1911; "What I Believe' published 1908;
'The Individual, Society, and the State' published 1940*

The Growing Discontent of the Masses: Three Essays on the Social Condition
Copyright © 2020 by VertVolta Press

All rights reserved. Published in the United States by VertVolta Press.
No part of this book's design may be reproduced in any manner
whatsoever without prior written permission.

Copy editing: Sarah Keliher

Book and Cover Design: Vladimir Verano, VertVolta Design

Front cover: Marco Verch, via Flickr.com, ⓒⓒ *v4.0*
Back cover: 'Brick damaged', via texturelib.com

print ISBN: 978-1-60944-139-5
ebook ISBN: 978-1-60944-140-1

VertVolta Press
3804 S.W. Admiral Way
Seattle, Washington 98126

vvdesignpress@gmail.com   www.vertvoltapress.com

Emma Goldman had a knack of speaking to the core of an issue, no matter how thorny.

She took on everything fearlessly: from the role of Theater in modern culture, to gender equality, workers' rights, political theory, social injustice, and more.

Because of this, Goldman's writings have attained a timelessness; sadly due to modern society's slow progress (and in many cases, regressions) of citizen's rights & freedoms.

These three essays address the current socio-political climate with Goldman's trademark dynamism, healthy skepticism, & hope.

On Patriotism

A Menace to Liberty

From *Anarchism and Other Essays*

Second Revised Edition. 1911

WHAT is patriotism? Is it love of one's birthplace, the place of childhood's recollections and hopes, dreams and aspirations? Is it the place where, in childlike naivety, we would watch the fleeting clouds, and wonder why we, too, could not run so swiftly? The place where we would count the milliard glittering stars, terror-stricken lest each one "an eye should be," piercing the very depths of our little souls? Is it the place where we would listen to the music of the birds, and long to have wings to fly, even as they, to distant lands? Or the place where we would sit at mother's knee, enraptured by wonderful tales of great deeds and conquests? In short, is it love for the spot, every inch representing dear and precious recollections of a happy, joyous, and playful childhood?

If that were patriotism, few American men of today could be called upon to be patriotic, since the place of play has been turned into factory, mill, and mine, while deafening sounds of machinery have replaced the music of the birds. Nor can we longer hear the tales of great deeds, for the stories our mothers tell today are but those of sorrow, tears, and grief.

What, then, is patriotism? "Patriotism, sir, is the last resort of scoundrels," said Dr. Johnson. Leo Tolstoy, the greatest anti-patriot of our times, defines patriotism as the principle that will justify the training of wholesale murderers; a trade that requires better equipment for the exercise of man-killing than the making of such necessities of life as shoes, clothing, and houses; a trade that guarantees better returns and greater glory than that of the average workingman.

Gustave Hervé, another great anti-patriot, justly calls patriotism a superstition—one far more injurious, brutal, and inhumane than religion. The superstition of religion originated in man's inability to explain natural phenomena. That is, when primitive man heard thunder or saw the lightning, he could not account for either, and therefore concluded that back of them must be a force greater than himself. Similarly he saw a supernatural force in the rain, and in the various other changes in nature. Patriotism, on the other hand, is a superstition artificially created and maintained through a network of lies and falsehoods; a superstition that robs man of his self-respect and dignity, and increases his arrogance and conceit.

Indeed, conceit, arrogance, and egotism are the essentials of patriotism. Let me illustrate. Patriotism assumes that our globe is divided into little spots, each one surrounded by an iron gate. Those who have had the fortune of being born on some particular spot, consider themselves better, nobler, grander, more intelligent than the living beings inhabiting any other spot. It is, therefore, the duty of everyone living on that chosen spot to fight, kill, and die in the attempt to impose his superiority upon all the others.

The inhabitants of the other spots reason in like manner, of course, with the result that, from early infancy, the mind of the child is poisoned with blood-curdling stories about the Germans, the French, the Italians, Russians, etc. When the child has reached manhood, he is thoroughly saturated with the belief that he is chosen by the Lord himself to defend *his* country against the attack or invasion of any foreigner. It is for that purpose that we are clamoring for a greater army and navy, more battleships and ammunition. It is for that purpose that America has within a short time spent four hundred million dollars. Just think of it—four hundred million dollars taken from the produce of *the people*. For surely it is not the rich who contribute to patriotism. They are cosmopolitans, perfectly at home in every land. We in

America know well the truth of this. Are not our rich Americans Frenchmen in France, Germans in Germany, or Englishmen in England? And do they not squander with cosmopolitan grace fortunes coined by American factory children and cotton slaves? Yes, theirs is the patriotism that will make it possible to send messages of condolence to a despot like the Russian Tsar, when any mishap befalls him, as President Roosevelt did in the name of *his* people, when Sergius was punished by the Russian revolutionists.

It is a patriotism that will assist the arch-murderer, Diaz, in destroying thousands of lives in Mexico, or that will even aid in arresting Mexican revolutionists on American soil and keep them incarcerated in American prisons, without the slightest cause or reason.

But, then, patriotism is not for those who represent wealth and power. It is good enough for the people. It reminds one of the historic wisdom of Frederick the Great, the bosom friend of Voltaire, who said: "Religion is a fraud, but it must be maintained for the masses."

That patriotism is rather a costly institution, no one will doubt after considering the following statistics. The progressive increase of the expenditures for the leading armies and navies of the world during the last quarter of a century is a fact of such gravity as to startle every thoughtful student of economic problems. It may be briefly indicated by dividing the time from 1881 to 1905 into five-year periods, and noting the disbursements of several great nations for army and navy purposes during the first and last of those periods. From the first to the last of the periods noted the expenditures of Great Britain increased from $2,101,848,936 to $4,143,226,885, those of France from $3,324,500,000 to $3,455,109,900, those of Germany from $725,000,200 to $2,700,375,600, those of the United States from $1,275,500,750 to $2,650,900,450, those of Russia from $1,900,975,500 to $5,250,445,100, those of Italy from $1,600,975,750 to $1,755,500,100, and those of Japan from $182,900,500 to $700,925,475.

The military expenditures of each of the nations mentioned increased in each of the five-year periods under review. During the entire interval from 1881 to 1905 Great Britain's outlay for her army increased fourfold, that of the United States was tripled, Russia's was doubled, that of Germany increased 35 per cent., that of France about 15 per cent., and that of Japan nearly 500 per cent. If we compare the expenditures of these nations upon their armies with their total expenditures for all the twenty-five years ending with 1905, the proportion rose as follows:

In Great Britain from 20 per cent. to 37; in the United States from 15 to 23; in France from 16 to 18; in Italy from 12 to 15; in Japan from 12 to 14. On the other hand, it is interesting to note that the proportion in Germany decreased from about 58 per cent. to 25, the decrease being due to the enormous increase in the imperial expenditures for other purposes, the fact being that the army expenditures for the period of 1901-5 were higher than for any five-year period preceding. Statistics show that the countries in which army expenditures are greatest, in proportion to the total national revenues, are Great Britain, the United States, Japan, France, and Italy, in the order named.

The showing as to the cost of great navies is equally impressive. During the twenty-five years ending with 1905 naval expenditures increased approximately as follows: Great Britain, 300 per cent.; France 60 per cent.; Germany 600 per cent.; the United States 525 per cent.; Russia 300 per cent.; Italy 250 per cent.; and Japan, 700 per cent. With the exception of Great Britain, the United States spends more for naval purposes than any other nation, and this expenditure bears also a larger proportion to the entire national disbursements than that of any other power. In the period 1881-5, the expenditure for the United States navy was $6.20 out of each $100 appropriated for all national purposes; the amount rose to $6.60 for the next five-year period, to $8.10 for the next, to $11.70 for the next, and to $16.40 for 1901-5. It is morally certain that the outlay for the current period of five years will show a still further increase.

The rising cost of militarism may be still further illustrated by computing it as a per capita tax on population. From the first to the last of the five-year periods taken as the basis for the comparisons here given, it has risen as follows: In Great Britain, from $18.47 to $52.50; in France, from $19.66 to $23.62; in Germany, from $10.17 to $15.51; in the United States, from $5.62 to $13.64; in Russia, from $6.14 to $8.37; in Italy, from $9.59 to $11.24, and in Japan from 86 cents to $3.11.

It is in connection with this rough estimate of cost per capita that the economic burden of militarism is most appreciable. The irresistible conclusion from available data is that the increase of expenditure for army and navy purposes is rapidly surpassing the growth of population in each of the countries considered in the present calculation. In other words, a continuation of the increased demands of militarism threatens each of those nations with a progressive exhaustion both of men and resources.

The awful waste that patriotism necessitates ought to be sufficient to cure the man of even average intelligence from this disease. Yet patriotism demands still more. The people are urged to be patriotic and for that luxury they pay, not only by supporting their "defenders," but even by sacrificing their own children. Patriotism requires allegiance to the flag, which means obedience and readiness to kill father, mother, brother, sister.

The usual contention is that we need a standing army to protect the country from foreign invasion. Every intelligent man and woman knows, however, that this is a myth maintained to frighten and coerce the foolish. The governments of the world, knowing each other's interests, do not invade each other. They have learned that they can gain much more by international arbitration of disputes than by war and conquest. Indeed, as Carlyle said, "War is a quarrel between two thieves too cowardly to fight their own battle; therefore they take boys from one village and another village, stick them into uniforms, equip them with guns, and let them loose like wild beasts against each other."

It does not require much wisdom to trace every war back to a similar cause. Let us take our own Spanish-American war, supposedly a great and patriotic event in the history of the United States. How our hearts burned with indignation against the atrocious Spaniards! True, our indignation did not flare up spontaneously. It was nurtured by months of newspaper agitation, and long after Butcher Weyler had killed off many noble Cubans and outraged many Cuban women. Still, in justice to the American Nation be it said, it did grow indignant and was willing to fight, and that it fought bravely. But when the smoke was over, the dead buried, and the cost of the war came back to the people in an increase in the price of commodities and rent—that is, when we sobered up from our patriotic spree it suddenly dawned on us that the cause of the Spanish-American war was the consideration of the price of sugar; or, to be more explicit, that the lives, blood, and money of the American people were used to protect the interests of American capitalists, which were threatened by the Spanish government. That this is not an exaggeration, but is based on absolute facts and figures, is best proven by the attitude of the American government to Cuban labor. When Cuba was firmly in the clutches of the United States, the very soldiers sent to liberate Cuba were ordered to shoot Cuban workingmen during the great cigarmakers' strike, which took place shortly after the war.

Nor do we stand alone in waging war for such causes. The curtain is beginning to be lifted on the motives of the terrible Russo-Japanese war, which cost so much blood and tears. And we see again that back of the fierce Moloch of war stands the still fiercer god of Commercialism. Kuropatkin, the Russian Minister of War during the Russo-Japanese struggle, has revealed the true secret behind the latter. The Tsar and his Grand Dukes, having invested money in Korean concessions, the war was forced for the sole purpose of speedily accumulating large fortunes.

The contention that a standing army and navy is the best security of peace is about as logical as the claim that the most peaceful citizen is he who goes about heavily armed. The experience of every-day life fully proves that the armed individual is invariably anxious to try his strength. The same is historically true of governments. Really peaceful countries do not waste life and energy in war preparations, With the result that peace is maintained.

However, the clamor for an increased army and navy is not due to any foreign danger. It is owing to the dread of the growing discontent of the masses and of the international spirit among the workers. It is to meet the internal enemy that the Powers of various countries are preparing themselves; an enemy, who, once awakened to consciousness, will prove more dangerous than any foreign invader.

The powers that have for centuries been engaged in enslaving the masses have made a thorough study of their psychology. They know that the people at large are like children whose despair, sorrow, and tears can be turned into joy with a little toy. And the more gorgeously the toy is dressed, the louder the colors, the more it will appeal to the million-headed child.

An army and navy represents the people's toys. To make them more attractive and acceptable, hundreds and thousands of dollars are being spent for the display of these toys. That was the purpose of the American government in equipping a fleet and sending it along the Pacific coast, that every American citizen should be made to feel the pride and glory of the United States. The city of San Francisco spent one hundred thousand dollars for the entertainment of the fleet; Los Angeles, sixty thousand; Seattle and Tacoma, about one hundred thousand. To entertain the fleet, did I say? To dine and wine a few superior officers, while the "brave boys" had to mutiny to get sufficient food. Yes, two hundred and sixty thousand dollars were spent on fireworks, theatre parties, and revelries, at a time when men, women, and child}en through the breadth and length of the country were starving in the streets; when thousands of unemployed were ready to sell their labor at any price.

Two hundred and sixty thousand dollars! What could not have been accomplished with such an enormous sum? But instead of bread and shelter, the children of those cities were taken to see the fleet, that it may remain, as one of the newspapers said, "a lasting memory for the child."

A wonderful thing to remember, is it not? The implements of civilized slaughter. If the mind of the child is to be poisoned with such memories, what hope is there for a true realization of human brotherhood?

We Americans claim to be a peace-loving people. We hate bloodshed; we are opposed to violence. Yet we go into spasms of joy over the possibility of projecting dynamite bombs from flying machines upon helpless citizens. We are ready to hang, electrocute, or lynch anyone, who, from economic necessity, will risk his own life in the attempt upon that of some industrial magnate. Yet our hearts swell with pride at the thought that America is becoming the most powerful nation on earth, and that it will eventually plant her iron foot on the necks of all other nations.

Such is the logic of patriotism.

Considering the evil results that patriotism is fraught with for the average man, it is as nothing compared with the insult and injury that patriotism heaps upon the soldier himself,—that poor, deluded victim of superstition and ignorance. He, the savior of his country, the protector of his nation,—what has patriotism in store for him? A life of slavish submission, vice, and perversion, during peace; a life of danger, exposure, and death, during war.

While on a recent lecture tour in San Francisco, I visited the Presidio, the most beautiful spot overlooking the Bay and Golden Gate Park. Its purpose should have been playgrounds for children, gardens and music for the recreation of the weary. Instead it is made ugly, dull, and gray by barracks,—barracks wherein the rich would not allow their dogs to dwell. In these miserable shanties soldiers are herded like cattle; here they waste their young days, polishing the boots and brass buttons of their superior officers. Here, too, I saw the distinction of classes: sturdy sons of a free Republic, drawn up in line like convicts, saluting every passing shrimp of a lieutenant. American equality, degrading manhood and elevating the uniform!

Barrack life further tends to develop tendencies of sexual perversion. It is gradually producing along this line results similar to European military conditions. Havelock Ellis, the noted writer on sex psychology, has made a thorough study of the subject. I quote: "Some of the barracks are great centers of male prostitution. ... The number of soldiers who prostitute themselves is greater than we are willing to believe. It is no exaggeration to say that in certain regiments the presumption is in favor of the venality of the majority of the men. ... On summer evenings Hyde Park and the neighborhood of Albert Gate are full of guardsmen and others plying a lively trade, and with little disguise, in uniform or out. ... In most cases the proceeds form a comfortable addition to Tommy Atkins' pocket money."

To what extent this perversion has eaten its way into the army and navy can best be judged from the fact that special houses exist for this form of prostitution. The practice is not limited to England; it is universal. "Soldiers are no less sought after in France than in England or in Germany, and special houses for military prostitution exist both in Paris and the garrison towns."

Had Mr. Havelock Ellis included America in his investigation of sex perversion, he would have found that the same conditions prevail in our army and navy as in those of other countries. The growth of the standing army inevitably adds to the spread of sex perversion; the barracks are the incubators.

Aside from the sexual effects of barrack life, it also tends to unfit the soldier for useful labor after leaving the army. Men, skilled in a trade, seldom enter the army or navy, but even they, after a military experience, find themselves totally unfitted for their former occupations. Having acquired habits of idleness and a taste for excitement and adventure, no peaceful pursuit can content them. Released from the army, they can turn to no useful work. But it is usually the social riff-raff, discharged prisoners and the like, whom either the struggle for life or their own inclination drives into the ranks. These, their military term over, again turn to their former life of crime, more brutalized and degraded than before. It is a well-known fact that in our prisons there is a goodly number of ex-soldiers; while, on the other hand, the army and navy are to a great extent plied with ex-convicts.

Of all the evil results I have just described none seems to me so detrimental to human integrity as the spirit patriotism has produced in the case of Private William Buwalda. Because he foolishly believed that one can be a soldier and exercise his rights as a man at the same time, the military authorities punished him severely. True, he had served his country fifteen years, during which time his record was unimpeachable. According to Gen. Funston, who reduced Buwalda's sentence to three years, "the first duty of an officer or an enlisted man is unquestioned obedience and loyalty to the government, and it makes no difference whether he approves of that government or not." Thus Funston stamps the true character of allegiance. According to him, entrance into the army abrogates the principles of the Declaration of Independence.

What a strange development of patriotism that turns a thinking being into a loyal machine!

In justification of this most outrageous sentence of Buwalda, Gen. Funston tells the American people that the soldier's action was "a serious crime equal to treason." Now, what did this "terrible crime" really consist of? Simply in this: William Buwalda was one of fifteen hundred people who attended a public meeting in San Francisco; and, oh, horrors, he shook hands with the speaker, Emma Goldman. A terrible crime, indeed, which the General calls "a great military offense, infinitely worse than desertion."

Can there be a greater indictment against patriotism than that it will thus brand a man a criminal, throw him into prison, and rob him of the results of fifteen years of faithful service?

Buwalda gave to his country the best years of his life and his very manhood. But all that was as nothing. Patriotism is inexorable and, like all insatiable monsters, demands all or nothing. It does not admit that a soldier is also a human being, who has a right to his own feelings and opinions, his own inclinations and ideas. No, patriotism can not admit of that. That is the lesson which Buwalda was made to learn; made to learn at a rather costly, though not at a useless price. When he returned to freedom, he had lost his position in the army, but he regained his self-respect. After all, that is worth three years of imprisonment.

A writer on the military conditions of America, in a recent article, commented on the power of the military man over the civilian in Germany. He said, among other things, that if our Republic had no other meaning than to guarantee all citizens equal rights, it would have just cause for existence. I am convinced that the writer was not in Colorado during the patriotic régime of General Bell. He probably would have changed his mind had he seen how, in the name of patriotism and the Republic, men were thrown into bull-pens, dragged about, driven across the border, and subjected to all kinds of indignities. Nor is that Colorado incident the only one in the growth of military power in the United States. There is hardly a strike where troops and militia do not come to the rescue of those in power, and where they do not act as arrogantly and brutally as do the men wearing the Kaiser's uniform. Then, too, we have the Dick military law. Had the writer forgotten that?

A great misfortune with most of our writers is that they are absolutely ignorant on current events, or that, lacking honesty, they will not speak of these matters. And so it has come to pass that the Dick military law was rushed through Congress with little discussion and still less publicity,—a law which gives the President the power to turn a peaceful citizen into a bloodthirsty man-killer, supposedly for the defense of the country, in reality for the protection of the interests of that particular party whose mouthpiece the President happens to be.

Our writer claims that militarism can never become such a power in America as abroad, since it is voluntary with us, while compulsory in the Old World. Two very important facts, however, the gentleman forgets to consider. First, that conscription has created in Europe a deep-seated hatred of militarism among all classes of society. Thousands of young recruits enlist under protest and, once in the army, they will use every possible means to desert. Second, that it is the compulsory feature of militarism which has created a tremendous anti-militarist movement, feared by European Powers far more than anything else. After all, the greatest bulwark of capitalism is militarism. The very moment the latter is undermined, capitalism will totter. True, we have no conscription; that is, men are not usually forced to enlist in the army, but we have developed a far more exacting and rigid force—necessity. Is it not a fact that during industrial depressions there is a tremendous increase in the number of enlistments? The trade of militarism may not be either lucrative or honorable, but it is better than tramping the country in search of work, standing in the bread line, or sleeping in municipal lodging houses. After all, it means thirteen dollars per month, three meals a day, and a place to sleep. Yet even necessity is not sufficiently strong a factor to bring into the army an element of character and manhood. No wonder our military authorities complain of the "poor material" enlisting in the army and navy. This admission is a very encouraging sign. It proves that there is still enough of the spirit of independence and love of liberty left in the average American to risk starvation rather than don the uniform.

Thinking men and women the world over are beginning to realize that patriotism is too narrow and limited a conception to meet the necessities of our time. The centralization of power has brought into being an international feeling of solidarity among the oppressed nations of the world; a solidarity which represents a greater harmony of interests between the workingman of America and his brothers abroad than between the American miner and his exploiting compatriot; a solidarity which fears not foreign invasion, because it is bringing all the workers to the point when they will say to their masters, "Go and do your own killing. We have done it long enough for you."

This solidarity is awakening the consciousness of even the soldiers, they, too, being flesh of the flesh of the great human family. A solidarity that has proven infallible more than once during past struggles, and which has been the impetus inducing the Parisian soldiers, during the Commune of 1871, to refuse to obey when ordered to shoot their brothers. It has given courage to the men who mutinied on Russian warships during recent years. It will eventually bring about the uprising of all the oppressed and downtrodden against their international exploiters.

The proletariat of Europe has realized the great force of that solidarity and has, as a result, inaugurated a war against patriotism and its bloody specter, militarism. Thousands of men fill the prisons of France, Germany, Russia, and the Scandinavian countries, because they dared to defy the ancient superstition. Nor is the movement limited to the working class; it has embraced representatives in all stations of life, its chief exponents being men and women prominent in art, science, and letters.

America will have to follow suit. The spirit of militarism has already permeated all walks of life. Indeed, I am convinced that militarism is growing a greater danger here than anywhere else, because of the many bribes capitalism holds out to those whom it wishes to destroy.

The beginning has already been made in the schools. Evidently the government holds to the Jesuitical conception, "Give me the child mind, and I will mould the man." Children are trained in military tactics, the glory of military achievements extolled in the curriculum, and the youthful minds perverted to suit the government. Further, the youth of the country is appealed to in glaring posters to join the army and navy. "A fine chance to see the world!" cries the governmental huckster. Thus innocent boys are morally shanghaied into patriotism, and the military Moloch strides conquering through the Nation.

The American workingman has suffered so much at the hands of the soldier, State and Federal, that he is quite justified in his disgust with, and his opposition to, the uniformed parasite. However, mere denunciation will not solve this great problem. What we need is a propaganda of education for the soldier: anti-patriotic literature that will enlighten him as to the real horrors of his trade, and that will awaken his consciousness to his true relation to the man to whose labor he owes his very existence. It is precisely this that the authorities fear most. It is already high treason for a soldier to attend a radical meeting. No doubt they will also stamp it high treason for a soldier to read a radical pamphlet. But, then, has not authority from time immemorial stamped every step of progress as treasonable? Those, however, who earnestly strive for social reconstruction can well afford to face all that; for it is probably even more important to carry the truth into the barracks than into the factory. When we have undermined the patriotic lie, we shall have cleared the path for that great structure wherein all nationalities shall be united into a universal brotherhood, —a truly FREE SOCIETY.

What I Believe

From *New York World*

July 19, 1908

"What I believe" has many times been the target of hack writers. Such blood-curdling and incoherent stories have been circulated about me, it is no wonder that the average human being has palpitation of the heart at the very mention of the name Emma Goldman. It is too bad that we no longer live in the times when witches were burned at the stake or tortured to drive the evil spirit out of them. For, indeed, Emma Goldman is a witch! True, she does not eat little children, but she does many worse things. She manufactures bombs and gambles in crowned heads. *B-r-r-r!*

Such is the impression the public has of myself and my beliefs. It is therefore very much to the credit of *The World* that it gives its readers at least an opportunity to learn what my beliefs really are.

The student of the history of progressive thought is well aware that every idea in its early stages has been misrepresented, and the adherents of such ideas have been maligned and persecuted. One need not go back two thousand years to the time when those who believed in the gospel of Jesus were thrown into the arena or hunted into dungeons to realize how little great beliefs or earnest believers are understood. The history of progress is written in the blood of men and women who have dared to espouse an unpopular cause, as, for instance, the black man's right to his body, or woman's right to her soul. If, then, from time immemorial, the New has met with opposition and condemnation, why should my beliefs be exempt from a crown of thorns?

"What I believe" is a process rather than a finality. Finalities are for gods and governments, not for the human intellect. While it may be true that Herbert Spencer's formulation of liberty is the most important on the subject, as a political basis of society, yet life is something more than formulas. In the battle for freedom, as Ibsen has so well pointed out, it is the *struggle* for, not so much the attainment of, liberty, that develops all that is strongest, sturdiest and finest in human character.

Anarchism is not only a process, however, that marches on with "sombre steps," coloring all that is positive and constructive in organic development. It is a conspicuous protest of the most militant type. It is so absolutely uncompromising, insisting and permeating a force as to overcome the most stubborn assault and to withstand the criticism of those who really constitute the last trumpets of a decaying age.

Anarchists are by no means passive spectators in the theatre of social development; on the contrary, they have some very positive notions as regards aims and methods.

That I may make myself as clear as possible without using too much space, permit me to adopt the topical mode of treatment of "What I Believe":

I. AS TO PROPERTY

"Property" means dominion over things and the denial to others of the use of those things. So long as production was not equal to the normal demand, institutional property may have had some *raison d'être.* One has only to consult economics, however, to know that the productivity of labor within the last few decades has increased so tremendously as to exceed normal demand a hundred-fold, and to make property not only a hindrance to human well-being, but an obstacle, a deadly barrier, to all progress. It is the private dominion over things that condemns millions of people to be mere nonentities, living corpses without originality or power of initiative, human machines of flesh and blood, who pile up mountains of wealth for others and pay for it with a gray, dull and wretched existence for themselves. I believe that there can be no real wealth, social wealth, so long as it rests on human lives—young lives, old lives and lives in the making.

It is conceded by all radical thinkers that the fundamental cause of this terrible state of affairs is (1) that man must sell his labor; (2) that his inclination and judgment are subordinated to the will of a master.

Anarchism is the only philosophy that can and will do away with this humiliating and degrading situation. It differs from all other theories inasmuch as it points out that man's development, his physical well-being, his latent qualities and innate disposition alone must determine the character and conditions of his work. Similarly will one's physical and mental appreciations and his soul cravings decide how much he shall consume. To make this a reality will, I believe, be possible only in a society based on voluntary co-operation of productive groups, communities and societies loosely federated together, eventually developing into a free communism, actuated by a solidarity of interests. There can be no freedom in the large sense of the word, no harmonious development, so long as mercenary and commercial considerations play an important part in the determination of personal conduct.

II. AS TO GOVERNMENT

I believe government, organized authority, or the State is necessary *only* to maintain or protect property and monopoly. It has proven efficient in that function only. As a promoter of individual liberty, human well-being and social harmony, which alone constitute real order, government stands condemned by all the great men of the world.

I therefore believe, with my fellow-Anarchists, that the statutory regulations, legislative enactments, constitutional provisions, are invasive. They never yet induced man to do anything he could and would not do by virtue of his intellect or temperament, nor prevented anything that man was impelled to do by the same dictates. Millet's pictorial description of "The Man with the Hoe," Meunier's masterpieces of the miners that have aided in lifting labor from its degrading position,

Gorki's descriptions of the underworld, Ibsen's psychological analysis of human life, could never have been induced by government any more than the spirit which impels a man to save a drowning child or a crippled woman from a burning building has ever been called into operation by statutory regulations or the policeman's club. I believe—indeed, I know—that whatever is fine and beautiful in the human expresses and asserts itself in spite of government, and not because of it.

The Anarchists are therefore justified in assuming that Anarchism—the absence of government—will insure the widest and greatest scope for unhampered human development, the cornerstone of true social progress and harmony.

As to the stereotyped argument that government acts as a check on crime and vice, even the makers of law no longer believe it. This country spends millions of dollars for the maintenance of her "criminals" behind prison bars, yet crime is on the increase. Surely this state of affairs is not owing to an insufficiency of laws! Ninety per cent of all crimes are property crimes, which have their root in our economic iniquities. So long as these latter continue to exist we might convert every lamp-post into a gibbet without having the least effect on the crime in our midst. Crimes resulting from heredity can certainly never be cured by law. Surely we are learning even to-day that such crimes can effectively be treated only by the best modern medical methods at our command, and, above all, by the spirit of a deeper sense of fellowship, kindness and understanding.

III. AS TO MILITARISM

I should not treat of this subject separately, since it belongs to the paraphernalia of government, if it were not for the fact that those who are most vigorously opposed to my beliefs on the ground that the latter stand for force are the advocates of militarism.

The fact is that Anarchists are the only true advocates of peace, the only people who call a halt to the growing tendency of militarism, which is fast making of this erstwhile free country an imperialistic and despotic power.

The military spirit is the most merciless, heartless and brutal in existence. It fosters an institution for which there is not even a pretense of justification. The soldier, to quote Tolstoi, is a professional man-killer. He does not kill for the love of it, like a savage, or in a passion, like a homicide. He is a cold-blooded, mechanical, obedient tool of his military superiors. He is ready to cut throats or scuttle a ship at the command of his ranking officer, without knowing or, perhaps, caring how, why or wherefore. I am supported in this contention by no less a military light than Gen. Funston. I quote from the latter's communication to the *New York Evening Post* of June 30, dealing with the case of Private William Buwalda, which caused such a stir all through the Northwest. "The first duty of an officer or enlisted man," says our noble warrior, "is unquestioning obedience and loyalty to the government to which he has sworn allegiance; it makes no difference whether he approves of that government or not."

How can we harmonize the principle of "unquestioning obedience" with the principle of "life, liberty and the pursuit of happiness"? The deadly power of militarism has never before been so effectually demonstrated in this country as in the recent condemnation by court-martial of William Buwalda, of San Francisco, Company A, Engineers, to five years in military prison. Here was a man who had a record of fifteen years of continuous service. "His character and conduct were unimpeachable," we are told by Gen. Funston, who, in consideration of it, reduced Buwalda's sentence to three years. Yet the man is thrown suddenly out of the army, dishonored, robbed of his chances of a pension and sent to prison. What was his crime? Just listen, ye freeborn Americans! William Buwalda attended a public meeting, and after the lecture he shook hands with the speaker. Gen. Funston, in his letter to the *Post,* to which I have already referred above, asserts that Buwalda's action was a "great military offense, infinitely worse than desertion." In another public statement, which the General made in Portland, Oregon, he said that "Buwalda's was a serious crime, equal to treason."

It is quite true that the meeting had been arranged by Anarchists. Had the Socialists issued the call, Gen. Funston informs us, there would have been no objection to Buwalda's presence. Indeed, the General says, "I would not have the slightest hesitancy about attending a Socialist meeting myself." But to attend an Anarchist meeting with Emma Goldman as speaker— could there be anything more "treasonable"?

For this horrible crime a man, a free-born American citizen, who has given this country the best fifteen years of his life, and whose character and conduct during that time were "unimpeachable," is now languishing in a prison, dishonored, disgraced and robbed of a livelihood.

Can there be anything more destructive of the true genius of liberty than the spirit that made Buwalda's sentence possible—the spirit of unquestioning obedience? Is it for this that the American people have in the last few years sacrificed four hundred million dollars and their hearts' blood?

I believe that militarism—a standing army and navy in any country—is indicative of the decay of liberty and of the destruction of all that is best and finest in our nation. The steadily growing clamor for more battleships and an increased army on the ground that these guarantee us peace is as absurd as the argument that the peaceful man is he who goes well armed.

The same lack of consistency is displayed by those peace pretenders who oppose Anarchism because it supposedly teaches violence, and who would yet be delighted over the possibility of the American nation soon being able to hurl dynamite bombs upon defenseless enemies from flying machines.

I believe that militarism will cease when the liberty-loving spirits of the world say to their masters: "Go and do your own killing. We have sacrificed ourselves and our loved ones long enough fighting your battles. In return you have made parasites and criminals of us in times of peace and brutalized us in times of war. You have separated us from our brothers and have made of the world a human slaughterhouse. No, we will not do your killing or fight for the country that you have stolen from us."

Oh, I believe with all my heart that human brotherhood and solidarity will clear the horizon from the terrible red streak of war and destruction.

IV. AS TO FREE SPEECH AND PRESS

The Buwalda case is only one phase of the larger question of free speech, free press and the right of free assembly.

Many good people imagine that the principles of free speech or press can be exercised properly and with safety within the limits of constitutional guarantees. That is the only excuse, it seems to me, for the terrible apathy and indifference to the onslaught upon free speech and press that we have witnessed in this county within the last few months.

I believe that free speech and press mean that I may say and write what I please. This right, when regulated by constitutional provisions, legislative enactments, almighty decisions of the Postmaster General or the policeman's club, becomes a farce. I am well aware that I will be warned of consequences if we remove the chains from speech and press. I believe, however, that the cure of consequences resulting from the unlimited exercise of expression is to allow more expression.

Mental shackles have never yet stemmed the tide of progress, whereas premature social explosions have only too often been brought about through a wave of repression.

Will our governors never learn that countries like England, Holland, Norway, Sweden and Denmark, with the largest freedom of expression, have been freest from "consequences"? Whereas Russia, Spain, Italy, France and, alas! even America, have raised these "consequences" to the most pressing political factor. Ours is supposed to be a country ruled by the majority, yet every policeman who is not vested with power by the majority can break up a meeting, drag the lecturer off the platform and club the audience out of the hall in true Russian fashion. The Postmaster General, who is not an elective officer, has the power to suppress publications and confiscate mail. From his decision there is no more appeal than from that of the Russian Czar. Truly, I believe we need a new Declaration of Independence. Is there no modern Jefferson or Adams?

V. AS TO THE CHURCH

At the recent convention of the political remnants of a once revolutionary idea it was voted that religion and vote getting have nothing to do with each other. Why should they? "So long as man is willing to delegate to the devil the care of his soul, he might, with the same consistency, delegate to the politician the care of his rights. That religion is a private affair has long been settled by the Bis-Marxian Socialists of Germany. Our American Marxians, poor of blood and originality, must needs go to Germany for their wisdom. That wisdom has served as a capital whip to lash the several millions of people into the well-disciplined army of Socialism. It might do the same here. For goodness' sake, let's not offend respectability, let's not hurt the religious feelings of the people.

Religion is a superstition that originated in man's mental inability to solve natural phenomena. The

Church is an organized institution that has always been a stumbling block to progress.

Organized churchism has stripped religion of its naïveté and primitiveness. It has turned religion into a nightmare that oppresses the human soul and holds the mind in bondage. "The Dominion of Darkness, as the last true Christian, Leo Tolstoi, calls the Church, has been a foe of human development and free thought, and as such it has no place in the life of a truly free people.

VI. AS TO MARRIAGE AND LOVE

I believe these are probably the most tabooed subjects in this country. It is almost impossible to talk about them without scandalizing the cherished propriety of a lot of good folk. No wonder so much ignorance prevails relative to these questions. Nothing short of an open, frank, and intelligent discussion will purify the air from the hysterical, sentimental rubbish that is shrouding these vital subjects, vital to individual as well as social well-being.

Marriage and love are not synonymous; on the contrary, they are often antagonistic to each other. I am aware of the fact that some marriages are actuated by love, but the narrow, material confines of marriage, as it is, speedily crush the tender flower of affection.

Marriage is an institution which furnishes the State and Church with a tremendous revenue and the means of prying into that phase of life which refined people have long considered their own, their very own most sacred affair. Love is that most powerful factor of human relationship which from time immemorial has defied all man-made laws and broken through the iron bars of conventions in Church and morality. Marriage is often an economic arrangement purely, furnishing the woman with a life-long life insurance policy and the man with a perpetuator of his kind or a pretty toy. That is, marriage, or the training thereto, prepares the woman for the life of a parasite, a dependent, helpless servant, while it furnishes the man the right of a chattel mortgage over a human life.

How can such a condition of affairs have anything in common with love? —with the element that would forego all the wealth of money and power and live in its own world of untrammeled human expression? But this is not the age of romanticism, of Romeo and Juliet, Faust and Marguerite, of moonlight ecstasies, of flowers and songs. Ours is a practical age. Our first consideration is an income. So much the worse for us if we have reached the era when the soul's highest flights are to be checked. No race can develop without the love element.

But if two people are to worship at the shrine of love, what is to become of the golden calf, marriage? "It is the only security for the woman, for the child, the family, the State." But it is no security to love; and without love no true home can or does exist. Without love no child should be born; without love no true woman can be related to a man. The fear that love is not sufficient material safety for the child is out of date. I believe when woman signs her own emancipation, her first declaration of independence will consist in admiring and loving a man for the qualities of his heart and mind and not for the quantities in his pocket. The second declaration will be that she has the right to follow that love without let or hindrance from the outside world. The third and most important declaration will be the absolute right to free motherhood.

In such a mother and an equally free father rests the safety of the child. They have the strength, the sturdiness, the harmony to create an atmosphere wherein alone the human plant can grow into an exquisite flower.

VII. AS TO ACTS OF VIOLENCE

And now I have come to that point in my beliefs about which the greatest misunderstanding prevails in the minds of the American public. "Well, come, now, don't you propagate violence, the killing of crowned heads and Presidents?" Who says that I do? Have you heard me, has any one heard me? Has anyone seen it printed in our literature? No, but the papers say so, everybody says so; consequently it must be so. Oh, for the accuracy and logic of the dear public!

I believe that Anarchism is the only philosophy of peace, the only theory of the social relationship that values human life above everything else. I know that some Anarchists have committed acts of violence, but it is the terrible economic inequality and great political injustice that prompt such acts, not Anarchism. Every institution to-day rests on violence; our very atmosphere is saturated with it. So long as such a state exists we might as well strive to stop the rush of Niagara as hope to do away with violence. I have already stated that countries with some measure of freedom of expression have had few or no acts of violence. What is the moral? Simply this: No act committed by an Anarchist has been for personal gain, aggrandizement or profit, but rather a conscious protest against some repressive, arbitrary, tyrannical measure from above.

President Carnot, of France, was killed by Caserio in response to Carnot's refusal to commute the death sentence of Vaillant, for whose life the entire literary, scientific and humanitarian world of France had pleaded.

Bresci went to Italy on his own money, earned in the silk weaving mills of Paterson, to call King Humbert to the bar of justice for his order to shoot defenseless women and children during a bread riot. Angelino executed Prime Minister Canovas for the latter's resurrection of the Spanish inquisition at Montjuich Prison. Alexander Berkman attempted the life of Henry C. Frick during the Homestead strike only because of his intense sympathy for the eleven strikers killed by Pinkertons and for the widows and orphans evicted by Frick from their wretched little homes that were owned by Mr. Carnegie.

Every one of these men not only made his reasons known to the world in spoken or written statements, showing the cause that led to his act, proving that the unbearable economic and political pressure, the suffering and despair of their fellow-men, women and children prompted the acts, and not the philosophy of Anarchism. They came openly, frankly and ready to stand the consequences, ready to give their own lives.

In diagnosing the true nature of our social disease I cannot condemn those who, through no fault of their own, are suffering from a wide-spread malady.

I do not believe that these acts can, or ever have been intended to, bring about the social reconstruction. That can only be done, first, by a broad and wide education as to man's place in society and his proper relation to his fellows; and, second, through example. By example I mean the actual living of a truth once recognized, not the mere theorizing of its life element. Lastly, and the most powerful weapon, is the conscious, intelligent, organized, economic protest of the masses through direct action and the general strike.

The general contention that Anarchists are opposed to organization, and hence stand for chaos, is absolutely groundless. True, we do not believe in the compulsory, arbitrary side of organization that would compel people of antagonistic tastes and interests into a body and hold them there by coercion. Organization as the result of natural blending of common interests, brought about through voluntary adhesion, Anarchists do not only not oppose, but believe in as the only possible basis of social life.

It is the harmony of organic growth which produces variety of color and form—the complete whole we admire in the flower. Analogously will the organized activity of free human beings endowed with the spirit of solidarity result in the perfection of social harmony—which is Anarchism. Indeed, only Anarchism makes non-authoritarian organization a reality, since it abolishes the existing antagonism between individuals and classes.

The Individual,
Society and the State

From *The Place of the Individual in Society*

pamphlet, Chicago, 1940

The minds of men are in confusion, for the very foundations of our civilization seem to be tottering. People are losing faith in the existing institutions, and the more intelligent realize that capitalist industrialism is defeating the very purpose it is supposed to serve.

The world is at a loss for a way out. Parliamentarism and democracy are on the decline. Salvation is being sought in Fascism and other forms of "strong" government.

The struggle of opposing ideas now going on in the world involves social problems urgently demanding a solution. The welfare of the individual and the fate of human society depend on the right answer to those questions. The crisis, unemployment, war, disarmament, international relations, etc., are among those problems.

The State, government with its functions and powers, is now the subject of vital interest to every thinking man. Political developments in all civilized countries have brought the questions home. Shall we have a strong government? Are democracy and parliamentary government to be preferred, or is Fascism of one kind or another, dictatorship—monarchical, bourgeois or proletarian—the solution of the ills and difficulties that beset society today?

In other words, shall we cure the evils of democracy by more democracy, or shall we cut the Gordian knot of popular government with the sword of dictatorship?

My answer is neither the one nor the other. I am against dictatorship and Fascism as I am opposed to parliamentary regimes and so-called political democracy.

Nazism has been justly called an attack on civilization. This characterization applies with equal force to every form of dictatorship; indeed, to every kind of suppression and coercive authority. For what is civilization in the true sense? All progress has been essentially an enlargement of the liberties of the individual with a corresponding decrease of the authority wielded over him by external forces. This holds good in the realm of physical as well as of political and economic existence. In the physical world man has progressed to the extent in which he has subdued the forces of nature and made them useful to himself. Primitive man made a step on the road to progress when he first produced fire and thus triumphed over darkness, when he chained the wind or harnessed water.

What role did authority or government play in human endeavor for betterment, in invention and discovery? None whatever, or at least none that was helpful. It has always been the individual that has accomplished every miracle in that sphere, usually in spite of the prohibition, persecution and interference by authority, human and divine.

Similarly, in the political sphere, the road of progress lay in getting away more and more from the authority of the tribal chief or of the clan, of prince and king, of government, of the State. Economically, progress has meant greater well-being of ever larger numbers. Culturally, it has signified the result of all the other achievements—greater independence, political, mental and psychic.

Regarded from this angle, the problems of man's relation to the State assumes an entirely different significance. It is no more a question of whether dictatorship is preferable to democracy, or Italian Fascism superior to Hitlerism. A larger and far more vital question poses itself: Is political government, is the

State beneficial to mankind, and how does it affect the individual in the social scheme of things?

The individual is the true reality in life. A cosmos in himself, he does not exist for the State, nor for that abstraction called "society," or the "nation," which is only a collection of individuals. Man, the individual, has always been and, necessarily is the sole source and motive power of evolution and progress. Civilization has been a continuous struggle of the individual or of groups of individuals against the State and even against "society," that is, against the majority subdued and hypnotized by the State and State worship. Man's greatest battles have been waged against man-made obstacles and artificial handicaps imposed upon him to paralyze his growth and development. Human thought has always been falsified by tradition and custom, and perverted false education in the interests of those who held power and enjoyed privileges. In other words, by the State and the ruling classes. This constant incessant conflict has been the history of mankind.

Individuality may be described as the consciousness of the individual as to what he is and how he lives. It is inherent in every human being and is a thing of growth. The State and social institutions come and go, but individuality remains and persists. The very essence of individuality is expression; the sense of dignity and independence is the soil wherein it thrives. Individuality is not the impersonal and mechanistic thing that the State treats as an "individual". The individual is not merely the result of heredity and environment, of cause and effect. He is that and a great deal more, a great deal else. The living man cannot be defined; he is the fountain-head of all life and all values; he is not a part of this or of that; he is a whole, an individual whole, a growing, changing, yet always constant whole.

Individuality is not to be confused with the various ideas and concepts of Individualism; much less with that "rugged individualism" which is only a masked attempt to repress and defeat the individual and his individuality So-called Individualism is the social and economic laissez faire: the exploitation of the masses by the classes by means of legal trickery, spiritual debasement and systematic indoctrination of the servile spirit, which process is known as "education." That corrupt and perverse "individualism" is the strait-jacket of individuality. It has converted life into a degrading race for externals, for possession, for social prestige and supremacy. Its highest wisdom is "the devil take the hindmost."

This "rugged individualism" has inevitably resulted in the greatest modern slavery, the crassest class distinctions, driving millions to the breadline. "Rugged individualism" has meant all the "individualism" for the masters, while the people are regimented into a slave caste to serve a handful of self-seeking "supermen." America is perhaps the best representative of this kind of individualism, in whose name political tyranny and social oppression are defended and held up as virtues; while every aspiration and attempt of man to gain freedom and social opportunity to live is denounced as "unAmerican" and evil in the name of that same individualism.

There was a time when the State was unknown. In his natural condition man existed without any State or organized government. People lived as families in small communities; They tilled the soil and practiced the arts and crafts. The individual, and later the family, was the unit of social life where each was free and the equal of his neighbor. Human society then was not a State but an *association*; a *voluntary* association for mutual protection and benefit. The elders and more experienced members were the guides and advisers of the people. They helped to manage the affairs of life, not to rule and dominate the individual.

Political government and the State were a much later development, growing out of the desire of the stronger to take advantage of the weaker, of the few against the many. The State, ecclesiastical and secular, served to give an appearance of legality and right to the wrong done by the few to the many. That appearance of right was necessary the easier to rule the people, because no government can exist without the consent of the people, consent open, tacit or assumed. Constitutionalism and democracy are the modern forms of that alleged consent; the consent being inoculated and indoctrinated by what is called "education," at home, in the church, and in every other phase of life.

That consent is the belief in authority, in the necessity for it. At its base is the doctrine that man is evil, vicious, and too incompetent to know what is good for him. On this all government and oppression is built. God and the State exist and are supported by this dogma.

Yet the State is nothing but a name. It is an abstraction. Like other similar conceptions—nation, race, humanity—it has no organic reality. To call the State an organism shows a diseased tendency to make a fetish of words.

The State is a term for the legislative and administrative machinery whereby certain business of the people is transacted, and badly so. There is nothing sacred, holy or mysterious about it. The State has no more conscience or moral mission than a commercial company for working a coal mine or running a railroad.

The State has no more existence than gods and devils have. They are equally the reflex and creation of man, for man, the individual, is the only reality. The State is but the shadow of man, the shadow of his opaqueness of his ignorance and fear.

Life begins and ends with man, the individual. Without him there is no race, no humanity, no State. No, not even "society" is possible without man. It is the individual who lives, breathes and suffers. His development, his advance, has been a continuous struggle against the fetishes of his own creation and particularly so against the "State."

In former days religious authority fashioned political life in the image of the Church. The authority of the State, the "rights" of rulers came from on high; power, like faith, was divine. Philosophers have written thick volumes to prove the sanctity of the State; some have even clad it with infallibility and with god-like attributes Some have talked themselves into the insane notion that the State is "superhuman," the supreme reality, "the absolute."

Enquiry was condemned as blasphemy. Servitude was the highest virtue. By such precepts and training certain things came to be regarded as self-evident, as sacred of their truth ,but [sic] because of constant and persistent repetition.

All progress has been essentially an unmasking of "divinity" and "mystery," of alleged sacred, eternal "truth"; it has been a gradual elimination of the abstract and the substitution in its place of the real, the concrete. In short, of facts against fancy, of knowledge against ignorance, of light against darkness.

That slow and arduous liberation of the individual was not accomplished by the aid of the State. On the contrary, it was by continuous conflict, by a life-and death struggle with the State, that even the smallest vestige of independence and freedom has been won. It has cost mankind much time and blood to secure what little it has gained so far from kings, tsars and governments.

The great heroic figure of that long Golgotha has been Man. It has always been the individual, often alone and singly, at other times in unity and co-operation with others of his kind, who has fought and bled in the age-long battle against suppression and oppression, against the powers that enslave and degrade him.

More than that and more significant: It was man, the individual, whose soul first rebelled against injustice and degradation; it was the individual who first conceived the idea of resistance to the conditions under which he chafed. In short, it is always the individual who is the parent of the liberating thought as well as of the deed.

This refers not only to political struggles, but to the entire gamut of human life and effort, in all ages and climes. It has always been the individual, the man of strong mind and will to liberty, who paved the way for every human advance, for every step toward a freer and better world; in science, philosophy and art, as well as in industry, whose genius rose to the heights, conceiving the "impossible," visualizing its realization and imbuing others with his enthusiasm to work and strive for it. Socially speaking, it was always the prophet, the seer, the idealist, who dreamed of a world more to his heart's desire and who served as the beacon light on the road to greater achievement.

The State, every government whatever its form, character or color—be it absolute or constitutional, monarchy or republic, Fascist, Nazi or Bolshevik—is by its very nature conservative, static, intolerant of change and opposed to it. Whatever changes it undergoes are always the result of pressure exerted upon it, pressure strong enough to compel the ruling powers to submit peaceably or otherwise, generally "otherwise"—that is, by revolution. Moreover, the inherent conservatism of government, of authority of any kind, unavoidably becomes reactionary. For two reasons: first, because it is in the nature of government not only to retain the power it has, but also to strengthen, widen and perpetuate it, nationally as well as internationally. The stronger authority grows, the greater the State and its power, the less it can tolerate a similar authority or political power along side of itself. The psychology of government demands that its influence and prestige constantly grow, at home and abroad, and it exploits every opportunity to increase it. This tendency is motivated by the financial and commercial interests back of the government, represented and served by it. The fundamental *raison d'etre* of every government to which, incidentally, historians of former days willfully shut their eyes, has become too obvious now even for professors to ignore.

The other factor which impels governments to become even more conservative and reactionary is their inherent distrust of the individual and fear of individuality. Our political and social scheme cannot afford to tolerate the individual and his constant quest for innovation. In "self-defense" the State therefore suppresses, persecutes, punishes and even deprives the individual of life. It is aided in this by every institution that stands for the preservation of the existing order. It resorts to every form of violence and force, and its efforts are supported by the "moral indignation" of the majority against the heretic, the social dissenter and the political rebel—the majority for centuries drilled in State worship, trained in discipline and obedience and subdued by the awe of authority in the home, the school, the church and the press.

The strongest bulwark of authority is uniformity; the least divergence from it is the greatest crime. The wholesale mechanization of modern life has increased uniformity a thousandfold. It is everywhere present, in habits, tastes, dress, thoughts and ideas. Its most concentrated dullness is "public opinion." Few have the courage to stand out against it. He who refuses to submit is at once labelled "queer," "different," and decried as a disturbing element in the comfortable stagnancy of modern life.

Perhaps even more than constituted authority, it is social uniformity and sameness that harass the individual most. His very "uniqueness," "separateness" and "differentiation" make him an alien, not only in his native place, but even in his own home. Often more so than the foreign born who generally falls in with the established.

In the true sense one's native land, with its back ground of tradition, early impressions, reminiscences and other things dear to one, is not enough to make sensitive human beings feel at home. A certain atmosphere of "belonging," the consciousness of being "at one" with the people and environment, is more essential to one's feeling of home. This holds good in relation to one's family, the smaller local circle, as well as the larger phase of the life and activities commonly called one's country. The individual whose vision encompasses the whole world often feels nowhere so hedged in and out of touch with his surroundings than in his native land.

In pre-war time the individual could at least escape national and family boredom. The whole world was open to his longings and his quests. Now the world has become a prison, and life continual solitary confinement. Especially is this true since the advent of dictatorship, right and left.

Friedrich Nietzsche called the State a cold monster. What would he have called the hideous beast in the garb of modern dictatorship? Not that government had ever allowed much scope to the individual; but the champions of the new State ideology do not grant even that much. "The individual is nothing," they declare, "it is the collectivity which counts." Nothing less than the complete surrender of the individual will satisfy the insatiable appetite of the new deity.

Strangely enough, the loudest advocates of this new gospel are to be found among the British and American intelligentsia. Just now they are enamored with the "dictatorship of the proletariat." In theory only, to be sure. In practice, they still prefer the few liberties in their own respective countries. They go to Russia for a short visit or as salesmen of the "revolution," but they feel safer and more comfortable at home.

Perhaps it is not only lack of courage which keeps these good Britishers and Americans in their native lands rather than in the millennium come. Subconsciously there may lurk the feeling that individuality remains the most fundamental fact of all human association, suppressed and persecuted yet never defeated, and in the long run the victor.

The "genius of man," which is but another name for personality and individuality, bores its way through all the caverns of dogma, through the thick walls of tradition and custom, defying all taboos, setting authority at naught, facing contumely and the scaffold—ultimately to be blessed as prophet and martyr by succeeding generations. But for the "genius of man," that inherent, persistent quality of individuality, we would be still roaming the primeval forests.

Peter Kropotkin has shown what wonderful results this unique force of man's individuality has achieved when strengthened by *co-operation* with other individualities. The one-sided and entirely inadequate Darwinian theory of the struggle for existence received its biological and sociological completion from the great Anarchist scientist and thinker. In his profound work, *Mutual Aid* Kropotkin shows that in the animal kingdom, as well as in human society, co-operation—as opposed to internecine strife and struggle—has worked for the survival and evolution of the species. He demonstrated that only mutual aid and voluntary co-operation—not the omnipotent, all-devastating State—can create the basis for a free individual and associational life.

At present the individual is the pawn of the zealots of dictatorship and the equally obsessed zealots of "rugged individualism." The excuse of the former is its claim of a new objective. The latter does not even make a pretense of anything new. As a matter of fact "rugged individualism" has learned nothing and forgotten nothing. Under its guidance the brute struggle for physical existence is still kept up. Strange as it may seem, and utterly absurd as it is, the struggle for physical survival goes merrily on though the necessity for it has entirely disappeared. Indeed, the struggle is being continued apparently because there is no necessity for it. Does not so-called overproduction prove it? Is not the world-wide economic crisis an eloquent demonstration that the struggle for existence is being maintained by the blindness of "rugged individualism" at the risk of its own destruction?

One of the insane characteristics of this struggle is the complete negation of the relation of the producer to the things he produces. The average worker has no inner point of contact with the industry he is employed in, and he is a stranger to the process of production of which he is a mechanical part. Like any other cog of the machine, he is replaceable at any time by other similar depersonalized human beings.

The intellectual proletarian, though he foolishly thinks himself a free agent, is not much better off. He, too, has a little choice or self-direction, in his particular metier as his brother who works with his hands. Material considerations and desire for greater social prestige are usually the deciding factors in the vocation of the intellectual. Added to it is the tendency to follow in the footsteps of family tradition, and become doctors, lawyers, teachers, engineers, etc. The groove requires less effort and personality. In consequence nearly everybody is out of place in our present scheme of things. The masses plod on, partly because their senses have been dulled by the deadly routine of work and because they must eke out an existence. This applies with even greater force to the political fabric of today. There is no place in its texture for free choice of independent thought and activity. There is a place only for voting and tax-paying puppets.

The interests of the State and those of the individual differ fundamentally and are antagonistic. The State and the political and economic institutions it supports can exist only by fashioning the individual to their particular purpose; training him to respect ''law and order;'' teaching him obedience, submission and unquestioning faith in the wisdom and justice of government; above all, loyal service and complete self-sacrifice when the State commands it, as in war. The State puts itself and its interests even above the claims of religion and of God. It punishes religious or conscientious scruples against individuality because there is no individuality without liberty, and liberty is the greatest menace to authority.

The struggle of the individual against these tremendous odds is the more difficult—too often dangerous to life and limb—because it is not truth or falsehood which serves as the criterion of the opposition he meets. It is not the validity or usefulness of his thought or activity which rouses against him the forces of the State and of "public opinion." The persecution of the innovator and protestant has always been inspired by fear on the part of constituted authority of having its infallibility questioned and its power undermined.

Man's true liberation, individual and collective, lies in his emancipation from authority and from the belief in it. All human evolution has been a struggle in that direction and for that object. It is not invention and mechanics which constitute development. The ability to travel at the rate of 100 miles an hour is no evidence of being civilized. True civilization is to be measured by the individual, the unit of all social life; by his individuality and the extent to which it is free to have its being to grow and expand unhindered by invasive and coercive authority.

Socially speaking, the criterion of civilization and culture is the degree of liberty and economic opportunity which the individual enjoys; of social and international unity and co-operation unrestricted by man-made laws and other artificial obstacles; by the absence of privileged castes and by the reality of liberty and human dignity; in short, by the true emancipation of the individual.

Political absolutism has been abolished because men have realized in the course of time that absolute power is evil and destructive. But the same thing is true of all power, whether it be the power of privilege, of money, of the priest, of the politician or of so-called democracy. In its effect on individuality it matters little what the particular character of coercion is—whether it be as black as Fascism, as yellow as Nazism or as pretentiously red as Bolshevism. It is power that corrupts and degrades both master and slave and it makes no difference whether the power is wielded by an autocrat, by parliament or Soviets. More pernicious than the power of a dictator is that of a class; the most terrible—the tyranny of a majority.

The long process of history has taught man that division and strife mean death, and that unity and cooperation advance his cause, multiply his strength and further his welfare. The spirit of government has always worked against the social application of this vital lesson, except where it served the State and aided its own particular interests. It is this anti-progressive and anti-social spirit of the State and of the privileged castes back of it which has been responsible for the bitter struggle between man and man. The individual and ever larger groups of individuals are beginning to see beneath the surface of the established order of things. No longer are they so blinded as in the past by the glare and tinsel of the State idea, and of the "blessings" of "rugged individualism." Man is reaching out for the wider scope of human relations which liberty alone can give. For true liberty is not a mere scrap of paper called "constitution," "legal right" or "law." It is not an abstraction derived from the non-reality known as "the State." It is not the *negative* thing of being free *from* something, because with such freedom you may starve to death. Real freedom, true liberty *is positive*: it is freedom *to* something; it is the liberty to be, to do; in short, the liberty of actual and active opportunity.

That sort of liberty is not a gift: it is the natural right of man, of every human being. It cannot be given: it cannot be conferred by any law or government. The need of it, the longing for it, is inherent in the individual. Disobedience to every form of coercion is the instinctive expression of it. Rebellion and revolution are the more or less conscious attempt to achieve it. Those manifestations, individual and social, are fundamentally expressions of the values of man. That those values may be nurtured, the community must realize that its greatest and most lasting asset is the unit—the individual.

In religion, as in politics, people speak of abstractions and believe they are dealing with realities. But when it does come to the real and the concrete, most people seem to lose vital touch with it. It may well be because reality alone is too matter-of-fact, too cold to enthuse the human soul. It can be aroused to enthusiasm only by things out of the commonplace, out of the ordinary. In other words, the Ideal is the spark that fires the imagination and hearts of men. Some ideal is needed to rouse man out of the inertia and humdrum of his existence and turn the abject slave into an heroic figure.

Right here, of course, comes the Marxist objector who has out-Marxed Marx himself. To such a one, man is a mere puppet in the hands of that metaphysical Almighty called economic determinism or, more vulgarly, the class struggle. Man's will, individual and collective, his psychic life and mental orientation count for almost nothing with our Marxist and do not affect his conception of human history.

No intelligent student will deny the importance of the economic factor in the social growth and development of mankind. But only narrow and willful dogmatism can persist in remaining blind to the important role played by an idea as conceived by the imagination and aspirations of the individual.

It were vain and unprofitable to attempt to balance one factor as against another in human experience. No one single factor in the complex of individual or social behavior can be designated as the factor of decisive quality. We know too little, and may never know enough, of human psychology to weigh and measure the relative values of this or that factor in determining man's conduct. To form such dogmas in their social connotation is nothing short of bigotry; yet, perhaps, it has its uses, for the very attempt to do so proved the persistence of the human will and confutes the Marxists.

Fortunately even some Marxists are beginning to see that all is not well with the Marxian creed. After all, Marx was but human—all too human—hence by no means infallible. The practical application of economic determinism in Russia is helping to clear the minds of the more intelligent Marxists. This can be seen in the transvaluation of Marxian values going on in Socialist and even Communist ranks in some European countries. They are slowly realizing that their theory has overlooked the human element, *den Menschen*, as a Socialist paper put it. Important as the economic factor is, it is not enough. The rejuvenation of mankind needs the inspiration and energizing force of an ideal.

Such an ideal I see in Anarchism. To be sure, not in the popular misrepresentations of Anarchism spread by the worshippers of the State and authority. I mean the philosophy of a new social order based on the released energies of the individual and the free association of liberated individuals.

Of all social theories Anarchism alone steadfastly proclaims that society exists for man, not man for society. The sole legitimate purpose of society is to serve the needs and advance the aspiration of the individual. Only by doing so can it justify its existence and be an aid to progress and culture.

The political parties and men savagely scrambling for power will scorn me as hopelessly out of tune with our time. I cheerfully admit the charge. I find comfort in the assurance that their hysteria lacks enduring quality. Their hosanna is but of the hour.

Man's yearning for liberation from all authority and power will never be soothed by their cracked song. Man's quest for freedom from every shackle is eternal. It must and will go on.

Born in Russia in 1869, EMMA GOLDMAN emigrated to the United States in 1885 to escape an arranged marriage. She soon found herself in the center of the various social activist movements pushing back against the plutocracy breaking the backs of workers across the U.S. and around the world.

Goldman became a highly sought-after lecturer on anarchist philosophy, women's rights, and social issues. Her sharp intellect and passion singled her out as a popular speaker; it was not uncommon for her events to draw thousands of listeners.

As her fame grew, so did her list of enemies—high society, wealthy industrialists, corrupt journalists, state and federal politicians. Goldman was arrested several times over the years for various reasons, including "inciting to riot" and illegally distributing information about birth control.

Eventually her activism led the U.S .Government to exile Goldman, along with Alexander Berkman and other dissidents, to Russia in 1921. Here she witnessed first-hand the brutality of the Communist experiment, which sparked her outspoken opposition to the Soviet regime.

Goldman was a prolific writer & publisher, founding the Mother Earth journal, and writing multiple pamphlets and articles for newspapers and magazines across the globe, as well as six books, including her expansive 2 volume memoir *Living My Life*, and the now-classic collection *Anarchism and Other Essays*.

Goldman spent the remainder of her life in exile from the U.S., living in various countries before eventually settling in Canada. She died in Toronto in 1940.

OTHER BOOKS BY VERTVOLTA PRESS

THE MIS-EDUCATION OF THE NEGRO, by Carter Godwin Woodson

978-1-60944-130-2, *$12.99*

ANARCHISM AND OTHER ESSAYS, by EMMA GOLDMAN

978-1-60944-113-5, $14.00

FLY TO THE ASSEMBLIES: *Seattle and the Rise of the Resistance*
edited by MARCUS HARRISON GREEN

978-1-60944-116-6, $15.99

EMERALD REFLECTIONS: *A* South Seattle Emerald *Anthology*
edited by MARCUS HARRISON GREEN

978-1-60944-109-8, *$17.00*

EMERALD REFLECTIONS 2: *A* South Seattle Emerald *Anthology*
edited by MARCUS HARRISON GREEN

978-1-60944-132-6, *$15.99*

Coming Soon

LIVING MY LIFE: A MEMOIR *Complete and Unabridged Edition*
by EMMA GOLDMAN

978-1-60944-141-8, *$TBD*

www.vertvoltapress.com

www.ingramcontent.com/pod-product-compliance
Lightning Source LLC
Chambersburg PA
CBHW020302030426
42336CB00010B/873